AF326784

GIVE ME A SIGN

A Sceptics Guide to Surviving Spiritual Awakening

J. H. F. Nichols

ISBN: 978-1-7641752-1-0

TABLE OF CONTENTS

Prologue

I was five years old. It was 1980, late August —cool and dry. The red desert sands rose up around me as if I were standing in a large crater. Dingoes rimmed the edge, advancing slowly with heads down, eyes fixed on their prey… me. Paralysed with fear and knowing it was a dream, but standing helpless, I could not wake. I would eventually feel their hungry breath in the moment before teeth met flesh.

I woke up screaming. My mother entered my bedroom shortly after. Both parents had spoken previously about this recurring nightmare. 'Maybe he'd seen the news on TV,' they reasoned. They made extra effort to keep me from hearing anything about Lindy

Chamberlain's case. You see, I had told them that the dingoes ate the baby.

Tonight, however, something different happened. My mother told me, "They are your dreams, Justin. You can control what happens." I'm sure I had been told the same or a similar thing before, but, for whatever reason, when I went back to sleep, I went straight back to the crater. This time, I wanted to go back.

There I was, and here they came. The fear that had gripped me so tightly before began its cold embrace. I remembered my mother's words, heard them echo in my mind: I know this is a dream—this is my dream. In a hail of bullets, I killed as many as I could. I waited until they were close, then opened fire as they fled up the sides to exit the crater, making them easier targets.

I awoke with a grin. No more dingoes were going to eat me. I snuggled up, rolled over, and had a good night's sleep for the first time in weeks. I remember I used Uzis—the '80s were a different time. Pretty brutal thoughts for a five-year-old. I still don't trust a lot of dogs.

Everything I discuss herein originated from this point. What my mother had inadvertently taught me that night was lucid dreaming. If there were a similar case today and I had dreams like this, I would be far more confident that I had somehow glimpsed the truth through my dreams. After ten hard years, Lindy Chamberlain was released from prison when evidence proved that dingoes had taken and killed her baby. A tragic story.

I would not doubt myself now.

Introduction

Interesting times we live in. It feels like all the blocks we have built reality on are being thrown high in the air. I think many of us feel it. I'm writing this book, because I feel I have to. What is written in these pages some will find hard to believe; others, I hope, will find something to relate to. Most of all, I want to help create hope for the future.

Who am I? My name is Justin Nichols, and I have some stories I'd like to share with you. I have a trade, and have successfully completed too many science subjects to write this story, yet here I am.

If you are into numerology, I'm double 11 for name and birth date, full birth name adds to 111. I realised that last one when I was double-checking my numerology. In Iridology, I'm a shaker; in astrology, Libra/Scorpio sun sign cusp, and it gets complicated. My palms tell a similar story. There appears to be consistency in archetypes using numbers and stars, as well as eye and palm patterns. Maybe there is some truth in the old divination tools, for all suggest I would have a mystical element to my life.

Sharing our unusual experiences, mystical moments and miracles, is frowned upon, for a number of reasons. Humility being one, it's easy to sound like you are boasting, like you are saying you are better in some way. It is even easier to sound like you are crazy. The truth is, because we all keep these moments secret, we have lost our shared experiences, we have lost our knowledge of the divine, the thread that connects us all.

I don't know what's going to happen, but it feels like things are reshaping. I want people to think hard about the future, I want people to realise that we do all have a connection to each other, and to all things. I hope that in sharing my stories, people can find something they feel an affinity too, a moment where an event I have been through triggers a memory of your own experience. I have come to believe this message is important. This is a monumentally important time in human history.

You are about to hear stories of psychic phenomena and uncanny coincidences that I struggle to believe: and they are my stories. Just a decade ago, I would never have shared these stories so publicly. Times have changed. This book runs on a timeline, and I have tried to focus on occurrences that included other people being present. If I refer to something like "my thoughts, or my new…" it is to be taken as at that time.. By no means are they all of my stories, but probably the most impactful. Shared experiences are harder to ignore. The names have been altered, but they are all real people, and confirmation could be sought in most cases. Given decades of these experiences including out of body experiences, seeing ghosts, prophetic visions, synchronicities with weather events, connections from previous lifetimes and even seemingly, time travel, I still have trouble accepting them. As you read these stories, know that I am being as honest as possible, the events are recorded as best as I can remember, with no embellishment. Most of us have received a phone call from someone we were just thinking of. It gives you the feeling they 'heard' you somehow. These phenomena are very real, they do happen, but we never really want to acknowledge it.

For those interested in the different phenomenon, I have included small sections throughout the book highlighting the lessons I learned. If it seems rushed, packed full, I apologise, I'm not a writer and this is my first attempt at compiling these events. Some events have taken my whole life to make sense, the meaning spanning decades from their initial occurrence. Bear with me. I hope I give a sense of what it has been like, the struggle with believing, and the realisation I should probably share my story and just accept it for how it is.

Buckle yourselves in: the opening story was just the beginning.

Inheritance

My parents are good people: my father, a Taurus, is analytical, dependable, and family-oriented. A surveyor of importance in a time without computers, mathematics was an integral part of his job. My mother, a Scorpio (many of my school friends called her 'Mum'), overflowed with love and intuitive wisdom. She just always seemed to say the right thing at the right time. When it came to answering questions about some of my unusual dreams, the advice from the two of them was distinctly different. While my father would conclude "It's just a nightmare or dream," my mother was more likely to share a story of her own. By the time I reached my teens, things had been getting much harder for my father to explain away.

We were driving to the Northern Territory from Queensland. My parents had told me they used to live in Darwin—they'd done this drive before. For anyone who isn't aware, when you're driving in a straight line for the majority of thirteen hours, that'll get you halfway. We were approaching a town when I excitedly announced, 'I've been here!'

'No, you haven't,' my parents replied in unison.

'Your brother wasn't even a glint in your father's eye,' Mum added.

I interrupted and said, 'I have been here. When we come into town, there's a big clock in the middle of a roundabout, with red and yellow flowers around it. We will have to turn right,' I said with conviction. Well, I wouldn't be telling this story if I hadn't been right. We entered the town and soon had to turn right. The clock and flowerbeds were as described. The silence in the car was unnerving. I sat back in my seat, feeling as though I had done something wrong.

My father spoke first. He explained that maybe it was something called déjà vu, where we get the feeling that something has happened before. My mother looked concerned. This was the first time I remember my father giving an explanation that was not backed by science. With all my siblings present, our parents told the following story:

'The last time we came here, we saw a min-min light.'

'A what?' we all chimed.

'A min-min light,' they replied.

'It's a ball of light seen in the Outback. Scientists think it might be ball lightning or gas,' my father added. Mum was giving him a look we were all familiar with—it generally meant you probably should not tell them this—but at the same time, she would like to tell us.

'Some people think they are UFOs,' he finished.

Understandably, my parents had all our attention, and we enquired further.

My father began, 'Well, it was just before dusk. At first, we thought it was Venus,'—my father always had an interest in astronomy—'people call it the evening star. It's the first to appear in our skies at night. After thinking about it, though, it was too low and not in the right direction. We thought maybe it was a reflection or distortion of headlights from a truck over the horizon.' The roads are so long and straight in this part of the country that they just disappear into the horizon. 'So we didn't worry about it for a while. After some time, it began to look as if it was on the road, so it was probably a truck with one light out, or a motorbike. We kept driving. As we got closer, we realised it wasn't coming toward us at all and thought perhaps it was a motorbike. When we caught up and went to pass it, however, it was just a light. We stopped the car. It stopped. I went to get out and have a closer look, but…'

Mum interrupted: 'I wasn't letting him get out!'

Dad smiled. 'She put her hand on my leg and said, "Don't you get out of the car, Maurie!"' He chuckled before continuing. 'I remembered a story I had heard about a group of blokes following one of those things. The only bloke who didn't go was charged with murder when they all went missing.'

'What happened then?' one of us asked, eager to hear more.

'Well, I shut the door and we drove off. We had the HQ doing about 150 k's an hour, and this thing just zipped up the road in front of us, disappearing. When we got further down the road—and your mother remembers this differently—there were a heap of cows on each side of the road, like a road train had ploughed them out of the way. We were going fast. If they had been on the road, we would have been in trouble.'

How had we never heard about this stuff?, I wondered. Having a story like this from our father—a practical man, an honest man, not prone to exaggerate or tell stories—I made a decision. Whatever had just happened to me was unusual; it had no explanation, and I wanted one.

On remote viewing

Looking back, I can see these moments for what they were. My father called it déjà vu, but it felt more active than that. As I grew, I realise these were glimpses, little remote viewing sessions. They are explorations of "I wonder" that can sometimes provide guidance. All I do now is close my eyes and relax. Your brain already knows what you seek—let it happen. My conscious mind only gets in the way. Driving in the car, dozing, thinking of where we are going, what we will see, the steady vibrations of the tyres on the road, the wind blowing somehow allowed me to travel ahead in my mind. When discussing this topic with my parents recently I was reminded of experiences they had shared under the same conditions. My mother used to dose, then wake and warn my father of

I wasn't going to ignore it. I didn't understand how difficult that would be at the time. I was just a boy full of curiosity. Explaining these things would require going down the rabbit hole…

Years passed. I'm sure there were many minor occurrences. I still had no idea just how different my perspective of the world was. Then, at the age of around fourteen, something changed. A separation from the norm.

It was dark. Night? Noisy? Wind and rain—was it a storm? I was on a ship, a wooden ship. My focus was drawn to a young girl, around the age of nine, standing in front of me. She was wet head to toe, dressed for sleep. She was trying to tell me something, yelling, but I could not hear her. The harder I tried to hear, the more distant the sound became…

I woke up wondering what on earth that was about—with the realisation I had been dreaming. It seemed the act of trying to listen with my ears made it harder to hear, ultimately waking myself up. It was very vivid. I recounted the events in my head and realised I had a date in mind—no doubt based on the attire and ship I had seen. I feel like it was just a year, not a day and a month. I honestly do not recall now. I also had an estimate of her age. Perhaps I had seen a movie recently? It didn't feel like a normal dream, though. It felt like it meant something.

Armed with these meagre clues and a puzzled face, I went to the breakfast table. By this stage, my family was used to hearing some pretty weird things, so I recounted my dream, the age, and the year. My family immediately set to task trying to help solve the mystery… over breakfast, of course.

My father suggested that perhaps the family tree might give us a clue. I wasn't aware at the time we had one in the house, or that it would date back that far. Alas, nothing relevant in the year I was looking for. It was a school day—

perhaps something would come up in class. I told the family not to worry, and we would just see what happens. At that point, my mother spoke: "I think my family tree goes back that far."

My mother then brought out a small booklet. It contained an exciting story of piracy and resistance against what is now known as Denmark. There she was—a girl aged nine who died at sea that year. Why would I need to know that? I was happy to learn about my ancestors on both sides, but it just didn't feel like that was all there was to it. Somewhat satisfied, somewhat bewildered, I started thinking 'Who am I?'

For my birthday that year, my eldest sister had the insight to buy me a set of Viking runes, and 'Who am I?' quickly changed to 'Know thyself.' I still use them on odd occasions today. Thanks, big sis!

That gift was more profound than she could have known. It was the beginning of understanding a fundamental truth: the world isn't as linear as we have been told. Memories of people from the past, like that girl, whom we have never met, should not exist. If you can be bothered looking however, there are many documented accounts of what seem impossible coincidences, children describing people's lives they did not know, with an accuracy that leaves little doubt that somehow, they connected with this 'memory'. Are they past lives? Are they just 'memories' we pick up for some reason? My intuition tells me it's the former. There are always more questions than answers in regards to the mysteries of life. Just try and accept the occurrence as it is, explanations often come with time, and it may take decades.

Discovery

My new motto, 'Know thyself,' is known for being written over the door to the Oracle of Delphi. I first came across it in the Book of Runes. It felt right, and things got stranger. Much stranger…

I got out of my bed, opened the bedroom door, turned right, and proceeded up the hallway to the lounge. Once I reached the lounge, I opened the front sliding door, walked across the verandah to the top of the stairs, and paused. What am I doing out here? I thought, feeling slightly alarmed. I must be sleepwalking. I could clearly remember walking out here—that's never happened before. Feeling concerned, looking down the stairs, and wondering why I had suddenly done this, I turned to go back inside. A cool, soft breeze blew from the direction of the stairs, and I began floating off the floor. My mind raced for an explanation. I was convinced I was awake, but being awake meant I was well aware I could not float. Quite the conundrum for a young mind! I could now feel the dew off the leaves of a tree I was brushing past as I slowly rose like a balloon to just below the rooftop. It has to be a dream, I decided. 'Wake up!' I yelled at myself repeatedly. It could only have been a second— it seemed longer—but I awoke. I was terrified, so scared I dared not move or make a sound. My eyes did not shut again that night. What just happened?

That was no dream. It was too real. I'm sure I felt things—like the door, the breeze—but I was asleep. There was a subtle difference—or was there? The light? Was it the same inside the house as outside? Something about colours— was it the light washing out colours? Was it just the moonlight?

Breakfast that morning saw an interesting discussion. It had to be a dream, just like nothing I had experienced before. My father was convinced it could be nothing else, and my mother found it interesting and concerning. She dreams a lot and she worries about her kids a lot —a recipe for many restless nights. I'm not sure I found 'just a dream' sufficient. Before liftoff, I was convinced I was awake. Then, only a few nights later…

I got out of my bed and walked to the bedroom door, put my hand on it, and… This is that freaky dream again! I thought to myself. I was still in my room. I turned, and I could see my brother and me lying in our beds. Yes, the light is different—it makes sense. My eyes are over there, shut. I looked peaceful. I felt peaceful. This is definitely the same place, I concluded. I crossed the room and sat on my bed before lying back down on myself. There was no break in consciousness—I just opened my eyes upon lying down. I felt much better. This time I felt I had some control. It certainly helped, being aware that it can happen in the first place. I hadn't heard of anything like this before.

Years later, I would discover the work of Robert Monroe and his book Journeys Out of the Body. His description of the world he was in was unmistakably the same place. I learned that what kept me wondering if these were more than just dreams were the thousands of documented Near-Death Experiences (NDEs). In NDEs, people report watching their own resuscitation from a corner of the room, hearing conversations they couldn't possibly have heard. The stories only really differ according to a person's core spiritual beliefs.

I realised I wasn't alone. I also learned that if you cannot lucid dream or remember your dreams, achieving this state consciously is difficult. I remember letting a vibration take over my body, syncing with it—just like tuning a radio. You don't mistake this type of dreaming for anything else.

At this point, I was lucid dreaming and having out-of-body experiences. I was also having prophetic dreams, which, in my own experience, is akin to remote viewing. I used to joke to my friends about being able to play any 'video' I wanted while I slept. I still did not have names for things that occurred, for example, I had never heard the term 'lucid dreaming, remote viewing, or out of body experiences'. While I realised out-of-body experiences weren't normal, I still hadn't realised most people couldn't remember their dreams, let alone alter or interact with them.

My parents, however, realised by now—after some interesting conversations at the breakfast table—and my uncanny ability to pick the card I wanted when splitting a deck of cards while playing Cribbage, that whatever was happening was beyond their capabilities to explain. I am quite certain they would have considered all possibilities. The thing was, I was just a normal kid. I was doing fine at school, had plenty of friends; I just had trouble with dreams. Sometimes they were prophetic, sometimes so real it seemed like I am walking around in the actual world. My parents didn't seem that concerned at all. My parents are Christians, non-practising, and I had religious education as part of school. For me, Christianity had contradictions that prevented me from embracing it. Some of it may be true, but it can't all be true. The result for someone like me is to move on, there must be a better answer, one with less contradiction. Regardless, I needed more information on what was happening to me.

The nearest city was around 100 kilometres away—I use the term "city" loosely, as the population was around 100,000. There was at least one bookshop, though, and my mother was keen to help me find some answers. I only remember there being one book that stood out, and I remember being disappointed and a little confused trying to find or explain the genre. I needed the book because I didn't know what people called any of it. It must have been somewhat embarrassing for my mother. The book I found, however, had a mostly red-coloured cover with a male and female sitting opposite each other, the man sitting with his legs crossed, their bodies surrounded by a light blue-hued glow. Today, half the world probably knows the lotus position. It sounds really corny and hard to believe for many, but I had never seen a picture like it. We bought the book. With hindsight, I wonder—considering my complete lack of knowledge on the topic—if it didn't have a picture conveying something like it did, I probably would not have found it. I distinctly remember it being in the "Fiction" section. It was a book on meditation and an absolute blessing.

I had heard about Buddhism and Taoism. I didn't really know anything about the practice of meditation, so I initially ignored it. The book contained chapters named 'Out-of-Body

Experience' and 'Astral Travelling.' These sounded like what I was looking for. I read it through once, skipping the meditations completely. I gave it a couple of days to sink in. This isn't fiction at all. With a "not sure how breathing can make a difference" attitude, accompanied by 'know thyself,' I gave it a go. Maybe I could learn something about myself.

Meditation

If you haven't learned how to belly breathe, please take the time.

When I first started, it was just simple colour meditations. Breathe in a colour, let it fill you from toes to head, breathe it out. It gives you a rinse. The only expectation you should have is to relax. An idiot has an empty mind—don't empty it, focus it. If you have an intruding thought, like a list of jobs for tomorrow, label it: 'That's a future-you problem. My problem now is to relax.' Then focus on your breathing. "Breathe in (through the nose).....Breathe out (through the mouth). Place a hand on your belly, when you take a deep breathe, you feel at the end of your breathe your stomach rise. This is your diaphragm, a muscle that pulls downwards on you lungs allowing it to fill with air. The trick is, don't move your chest, just your diaphragm, it takes a little practice, but it is not difficult given practice. You are the teacher and the student.

As a boy in the place and time it occurred, meditating was not normal. I didn't tell anyone. My family didn't tell anyone. I would have to teach myself, and I would be alone in my experiences, as I already was in my dreaming. To avoid making it weird, I mainly did it in my bed just before sleep.

I received insight upon learning to belly breathe. All those years before—the dingoes, my mother's conversation, my unfathomable belief in my mother's wisdom at such a young age—I had an answer. I had opened a door after that experience.

While things had happened leading up to that moment, a path between my conscious and unconscious mind had now been forged. That pathway had allowed me to lucid dream. Without it, you can't have a conscious out-of-body experience. You may still have them, and what you learn may still help you unconsciously. My example was the experience of knowing a place I hadn't been to. I believe I had dreamt it—I just hadn't remembered the dream until we approached. I could not, however, find the answers I was looking for, the person who had written the book was not convincing on the topic of out-of-body experiences.

I could not be sure it was the same thing described.

The section on astral travelling was useful. I would put it under the banner of remote viewing today. I know some people use the term interchangeably with OBE, for me, there has always been a distinct difference between an OBE, and any other type of dream state. I was also beginning to understand how much of what I considered normal was not normal at all. Why was I having experiences sort by readers of this book? While meditation is great, it must not be necessary to have them. It was quite exciting.

The Search for Secrets

By now, I was experimenting quite a bit without instruction. Not ideal. My third out-of-body experience—I sat on the side of my bed, next to myself, and juggled three balls of light. I can't juggle in real life, so that was pretty cool!

What could I deduce from my experiences at this time? Not a lot, but it was very peculiar. I seemed to be fully conscious outside of my body. I also seemed to be able to make things appear and move, like in a lucid dream. Things seemed far more real, however. It was exciting and concerning. I began using meditation before bed as a safeguard against other entities.

I hadn't met any—but better to be safe, as they are mentioned in various religions and texts on spirituality.

The only thing that kept me thinking I may not be crazy was those moments when you know without knowing. I was still living at home at this stage, sixteen to seventeen years old. We had a cat—he was a big cat, a stray we took in. I named him Jinx. My mother refused to call him that; she preferred 'Blacky.' His bright green eyes and two white canines protruding from his grin were in deep contrast to his jet-black fur. This cat was terrifying. He would ambush my friends as they came up the front stairs, reaching out through the steps before grabbing and biting their ankles. He was pretty cool. My older brother and I were the only ones who gave him many pats, but not without risk of a little blood.

At the time, going through puberty and dealing with the fact that witchcraft, prayer, and meditation are all linked somehow, Jinx's prickly nature suited me. That said, you could not trust this guy, and eventually I got annoyed.

I was playing in the backyard in the shade of our two-story house. Jinx came over and was rubbing up against my leg, so I bent down to give him a stroke behind his ear. He immediately twisted his head and front paws around, latching onto my arm and biting hard on my hand. Before I could react, he was now raking my forearm with his rear legs as well. Ignoring the pain I was in, I grabbed the back of his neck with my free hand and bent it until it snapped, throwing the cat on the ground. Then I woke up. This was a lucid dream, not an out-of-body experience, most likely because of the fear instilled by the cat. All that 'know thyself' had taught me something. He never bit or scratched me again, however. Perhaps he no longer could smell fear on me? Except, he didn't tell me he wasn't going to bite or scratch me again, so I was just as concerned as I was previous to having the dream. He also began waiting for me to come home—he would wait in my parking spot, somehow knowing the difference between a Friday and any other day of the week. Strange cat. I felt connected to this cat. When I'd come home, we would sit together at the top of the steps—after he would move out of my spot in the driveway, of course —just being, just observing the world together.

Insight comes from strange places. Jinx taught me something: 'Notice the butterflies.' It's a saying I would tell people who wanted to get a glimpse into the mysteries they may have experienced themselves.

The principle is simple. Noticing the butterflies and I do mean butterflies, not a metaphor, just notice them, see them, and acknowledging them, brings YOU into the present. It seems many today confuse living in the moment with a rush of adrenaline… that will not produce the intended effect. Stay present—that is the goal.

You can do that anywhere, doing any task. If you can't learn to be present, you may not even notice the odd coincidences we all experience. As most readers will know, there are a lot of distractions for those between the ages of sixteen and their early twenties. I was trying to be as normal as possible, but occasionally I would get caught out. A conversation with a friend where I would start talking about a secret of theirs we had spoken about the day before, the perplexed look on their face as they ask me how I would know that. I explain that they told them yesterday, and they insist no conversation of the sort took place. Awkward. No explanation, other than coming from a dream I had thought was real. Apparently, the universe was far from done messing with my head.

I wouldn't even tell this story if I weren't with someone at the time it occurred. One time, my friends and I were going fishing and camping for the weekend. To get to where we were staying required a half-hour boat trip across the ocean. We typically did this in a fourteen- to sixteen-foot aluminium boat. Because of the ocean crossing, we would always check the weather before going on such a trip. The weather was good—off we went. The moon was full, so there was plenty of light that night. We had a few cheeky beers, and I walked the short distance from the front of the beach hut to the waterline. Some places feel magical.

This place was like that—the moon bright, the water gently lapping against the shore, the phosphorus giving a faint green glow with the movement. Not sure why I chose to do this now.

I had got the impression that the runes, the symbols, had an energy to them, not just a meaning. Now seemed as good a time as any to do a little experiment. I intuitively cast a spell by scratching the runes I felt would make it rain into the sand. As I finished, one of my mates—who knew I was a bit odd—came down to investigate. I told him I was just trying something out before chuckling a little awkwardly: we were both under the effects of alcohol. He will forget it even happened, were my thoughts. It started spitting.

The shower turned into a downpour. The next morning, we had to leave as it was only going to worsen, so off we went into the boat, wind blowing up the waves and the rain pouring down. I couldn't help but wonder: Did I do that? Nah, that is crazy talk. Must be a coincidence. A week or more later, when it finally stopped, and the whole district was flooded, my friend who doesn't believe this stuff approached me. He hadn't forgotten what I had said, or what he saw scratched in the sand. He said, "I don't know what you did, but don't do that again." I didn't want to talk about it, but I thought that sounded like good advice. I was clinging to the idea it was just a coincidence. Hearing someone else suggest my fears was not comforting.

The dreams continued, so did the coincidences.

I had moved out of home for the first time, and now I found myself having out of body experiences in a new location. I woke to the sound of a rock hitting my bedroom window.

I jumped out of bed and looked out. A couple of houses away, there was an odd ball of light just a couple of feet off the rooftop. It looked very much like a streetlight, but the feeling I had was unnerving. Within seconds, an ear-piercing ringing in my head dropped me to my knees. I knew it was from the light. I was kneeling between the wall and my bed, hands over my ears, barely able to muster a thought. I suddenly realised I was out of my body—the noise at the window had not physically woken me up. I remember reading somewhere that if I were in trouble, I could call for help. So I did. Almost immediately, what appeared to be my flatmate in astral form entered my room. The sound ceased, and the light was gone. I woke after a restless night's sleep. My flatmate did not have any strange dreams she could recall. While I had moved out of my home, I was still in the same small town with not a lot of people I could talk to about these things. It just so happened, however, that a tradesman who occasionally worked with us was in town. He was a Pacific Islander—I knew he was a little more open than most, so I shared my experience. He promptly informed me he knows the people who live at the house where the light had appeared and added they were having a séance. Just a coincidence?

That was the only time I remember consciously calling for help and having it appear so readily. It solidified another lesson: if you encounter something malevolent, just remember: its opposing force exists as well. Ask for help if you need it.

That was the only time I remember starting an out of body experience in my room after moving out. When I exited my body, I might find myself anywhere. I had seemingly no control over when it would happen or where I would end up. More than half my experiences were spent battling demons—I figured they were probably the astral embodiment of my own very real fears. I learned more about that place doing that than any other way. Perhaps now is not the time for those stories. Where were all the guides people spoke of?

I tried to be normal. I tried to ignore the out of body experiences and odd synchronicities. To some reading this, that may sound strange. It didn't matter though. One night, I fell asleep after drinking at my sister's house. Do you know how your head spins when you have had too many drinks once you lay down? I was able to experience that out of my body before crashing into the ceiling, waking like I had just had a bucket of water poured over me. Not a lot of fun. In fact, the excitement of it all was sort of wearing off. It had been years, and I still had not come across any real information about out-of-body experiences. I was pretty sure I wasn't crazy, but I was tired. I was becoming reluctant to sleep on my back, just to try and ensure I could sleep the night through undisturbed.

My best friend at the time had given me a glimmer of hope. He loaned me a novel—the first in the Wheel of Time series by Robert Jordan. He obviously recognised my description of the dreams, described in the pages. I agreed with his assessment after reading them, it certainly appeared to us, Robert Jordan had either had an out-of-body experience or was close to someone who did. While the book was obviously fantasy, the description of 'The world of dreams' he gave, was the closest yet to the 'world' or place I was visiting. Someone out there had the information I was looking for. Other people were having these experiences. They were also keeping it to themselves.

Necessity and New Beginnings

I was now a qualified tradesman and was with a nice girl. Life was pretty good, but despite my efforts to ignore it all, things just kept happening.

I was in my car—a 1975 Chrysler Centura—pulling up next to what looked like ringers' quarters on a cattle station. My girlfriend at the time lived with her parents on the cattle station their family owned, but this wasn't it. There were two chairs and four people: two girls and two boys. I immediately noticed my girlfriend was one of them, sitting on someone's lap. I didn't know him.

I woke, feeling like my partner had cheated on me. I had visited people before in dreams, even waking a friend's brother at a specified time as an experiment, though the brother wasn't aware of the experiment beforehand. It appeared to work, though it could have been a coincidence. But had I really seen my girlfriend with another man? I couldn't shake the feeling. By now, the difference between types of dreams was pretty clear.

I can't recall if I told her about it or not, but it led to a breakup. The problem was, I could not convince myself it was just a 'dream'. We ended up back together after she turned up at a fancy dress party dressed as a nun. Twelve months later, my girlfriend came in for the weekend with a friend. Yep, I recognised him straight away. He lived on the cattle station next to hers. That night we went out together with her sister (my housemate) and her partner, and their cousin. I felt completely betrayed and retired early. When you feel like you are the last to find out, but you may have also been the first. They were married twelve months later. Still happily married.

Sometimes the coincidences hurt. I stopped thinking of them as gifts. I lost more than one person I cared about that day. Her sister was one of my closest friends. I'd lived with her for years, and she must have known if it happened, she was there in the dream to. I can't blame her for not ousting her sister, but it hurt. I never confirmed anything happened while we were together. I held no bad blood; but it's a small place, and I no longer felt like I belonged.

Time to move. I was off to the big smoke as fate would have it. By chance, my younger sister had taken a job in Melbourne. It was better than staying where I was. Looking back, I feel sorry for her, but most of all grateful. I was a bit lost for a while.

I tried working as a printing machinist, the trade I had acquired, but the first company I worked for went bust within a couple of months, and it was a fairly large company. That was a bummer. The previous business model for printing companies was changing; colour photocopiers had arrived. The end of most print shops was inevitable. I didn't see a future for me in it.

What to do? Well, perhaps I could use my knack for sparking coincidences or 'knowing' things I shouldn't. Perhaps I should try to get some answers. There was still no internet as we know it today, it was hard to come by and little was known by the public about what it could even do. Melbourne was multicultural and the second-biggest city in Australia. There had to be someone here who knew what was going on.

The two options I landed on were an intelligence officer for the Australian Air Force or a student of natural medicine. I'd always enjoyed tactical thinking games like chess, and I had extended family members who'd done well in the Air Force. I was pretty keen on the idea. Of course, the lure of 'being a hero' also played a role for a young male.

Just one thing kept popping into my head: while I could save lives doing either, I was only interested in defending Australia from aggressors. My historical knowledge of military conflicts taught me that wouldn't be the case. Although I'd started the process, I never showed up for the physical. A year later, the First Gulf War started, and shortly after, Australian aid workers were captured and accused of being intelligence officers. I felt like that was probably true—just a feeling, though.

As for natural medicine, I figured I could meet some weirdos there. Some of the subjects covered counselling and psychology—I could find out if I were crazy or not! Nothing is ever so black and white, though. I didn't have a great deal of faith in doctors. I couldn't get a diagnosis for a mysterious illness that would come and go over a five-day period every six months. This had gone on for years. After moving and no longer being exposed to the chemicals used in the printing process, it never happened again. The choice seemed obvious, so I enrolled in   a Bachelor of Health Science

(Naturopathy).

By this time, I'd worked out a few things. It appeared our body was just a vehicle, and the longer I'd spent with someone, the stronger a connection grew in some still-unexplained way.

A good example was when my grandfather had a heart attack. I was living with my sister when I had the overwhelming feeling that something bad had just happened. The feeling was strong enough that I told my sister exactly that: 'Something bad just happened.' Shortly after, the phone rang. It was my mother, informing us of the news. While I loved my grandfather, I didn't see him often. The feeling I'd had was due to my mother's reaction.

I'd also learned you could create some pretty unexplainable coincidences. While I initially believed ceremony and ritual were necessary, I'd generated the same results without them. Ritual, ceremony, chanting—they're aids, a key for a door you keep locked. This realisation was a turning point. It helped me see the common thread running through all cultures and belief systems.

On Connection and Belief

In the West, it's called 'vital force'. In the East: chi. Another name: mana. The Sanskrit name: prana. There's some force connecting all things. Miracles are present in every culture, attributed to all manner of beliefs. This means that faith, or belief itself, is a necessary component. Your beliefs are your keys to God. Everyone's key is slightly different. If your prayers or wishes are being answered, do not change a thing. Embrace it—it's your doorway. When dealing with those who seem to have opposing beliefs, remind yourself they just want to be closer to the source. Let them take their own path and wish them well on their journey.

I lost my luck, so to speak, as a result of this realisation… After meditating for some time… things went back to normal, it took months.

God, if such a thing exists, has to be connected to everyone. Perhaps, what we are told is a misguided version of the truth? My consciousness can be anywhere, but not everywhere at once; and God (whatever that may be) is supposedly everywhere at once. Is our combined consciousness God? Not a man, but more like a medium that permeates the entire universe. I had noticed a few things with magnets. If you smash a magnet to pieces, you just get more magnets. If you then put them back together, you have lots of bits, but one magnetic field. Consciousness and gravity, for that matter, may work the same way. So many questions.

These questions led me down a rabbit hole of research that would take years to synthesise. I learned I wasn't alone in my thinking.

Neuroscientist Jacobo Grinberg and his Syntergic theory proposes a model where everything in existence is connected by a lattice, enabling us to receive and transmit information instantaneously. Michael Persinger's work suggests a combined consciousness stored in the Earth's magnetic field. The similarities between these modern theories and the principles of the oldest religions are what you should focus on. We are connected, and we can tap into this information field—universal consciousness, God, divinity, the ether. The name doesn't matter.

The Student

As I expected, I met many people who were far more open to talking about what was largely a burden I kept to myself. Many of my friends in Melbourne may remember me saying on multiple occasions that these weren't 'gifts.' While many people I met there had stories to share of their own, which made me feel a little less nervous about the whole thing, I quickly noticed a pattern. People asked me for my thoughts, my interpretations. This was a bit strange, a nervous empowerment of sorts. Everyone kept asking me if I'd read The Celestine Prophecy. It must have come out in the mid-to-late '90s. I'd never heard of it. It was twenty years later before I would read the books, and then it was obvious why people asked the question. No doubt, some wished for my experiences and some questioned my authenticity.

I'd also noticed very few people were having out-of-body experiences, well, recalling them anyway—one person here and there, with a single story that had enough detail. I figured if you hadn't had them often, some of those people may have confused it for lucid dreaming or a 'vision'. It feels like it has meaning to them. Not all my out-of-body experiences felt like they had a meaning. Vivid dreams were a different story.

A tertiary-level learning environment is a truly special experience. Surrounded by like-minded people, learning becomes easy. I was able to access many books from libraries and friends. Learning how to heal illness—not just treat symptoms—I enjoyed the content; but it wasn't really why I was there. I learned a bit more about astrology and numerology through friends, counselling, psychology, and Iridology at college. They all talked in archetypes.

I'd spent many years trying to "know thyself" and liked to believe I had a pretty good grasp on who I was. I didn't feel I fit into one archetype, though—it seemed I was a mix. I put this down to the "know thyself" philosophy and meditation.

I was fairly outspoken during lectures, answering and asking a lot of questions—the annoying one. Our lectures were three hours long (online didn't exist) and I was "present" during class because I also had to work. Travelling on the train was pretty much the only time I would get to study.

On top of being annoying, I was given an opportunity to speak about some things I'd learned in a psychology class. This was the first time I would openly mention some of my experiences.

The time allocated was twenty minutes, with questions. The topic I was delivering was something along the lines of 'The Use of Runes as a Tool in Psychology.' I'd spent around five years working with them by now and had found them very useful.

I mentioned the out-of-body experiences and how they had led people to give me esoteric books and items over the years. I talked about the symbolism of the runes, how they're used everywhere, and how deeply connected we all are to some of the symbols. I also explained how our thoughts govern our perspective. This can be concluded by reading the same rune on a different day—different aspects of the rune's description jump out at you. This isn't a spiritual experience; this relates directly to your perspective at the time. The runes can tell you how you're thinking, the outcomes you want to hear, and your fears. They're a window into who you are. What stands out is just a reflection of 'you'.

While I have five sets of tarot/spirit cards given to me over the years, I used them less than runes, but found them to be the same, in that they allow you to recognise your perspective on the chosen matter. That said—and this is important to note—until you turn that card or rune, it can be any card or rune. Uncanny things will happen. I believe you can get spiritual messages this way… you just laugh when you get a 'bad' reading, because you understand why it appears bad…

This understanding of divination tools as personal mirrors is central to a larger truth about religion and belief. They both give you structure to work within, which can be very useful. If you are a Buddhist monk and have an out-of-body experience, it's seen as growth. If you see dead people as a devout Christian, it's a gift from God. The obvious benefit is finding your people. Having said that, dogma may limit your innate abilities.

There are many roads, and eventually we all meet.

Back to the story: twenty minutes were up, the class was pretty engaged, just a few questions… At thirty minutes, I turned to the lecturer and referred back to the class, suggesting my time was up and I should probably sit down. The lecturer replied, "While your peers have questions, you may continue"—not exactly what I wanted to hear. An hour and a half in, I was relieved to hear a break in questions.

The lecturer approached me after class and was interested in what my future plans were. I had no idea, to be honest, but she didn't seem to think I was crazy. That was good.

Now, a different class: Iridology. Time to test the content. I'm pretty sceptical about these things, despite my experiences. I didn't want this lecturer to know a thing about me—let's see if this Iridology has any merit.

We did our own analysis before passing our photos around. To be a bit clearer, you take a side-lit photo of your iris. By doing this, you can see different shapes and patterns more clearly. There are a number of basic patterns and shapes that relate to archetypes; these archetypes, when mixed, produce other sub-traits. If you have an even distribution of base archetypes, you are what's referred to as a 'shaker'. These are supposed to be change-makers.

Now, if the only class you had me in was this one, you would not think I was a shaker. If you had me in any other class, particularly if you'd heard my presentation on runes, then yeah, you may suspect a shaker. As it turned out, I was a shaker. Despite meeting the physical patterns required the lecturer did not agree, she said, 'We would know if he was a shaker'—which got a few chuckles from my peers. I have no doubt my peers had wondered why I was being so quiet for a change. Now they knew. Maybe I do have an archetype.

So I am a shaker in Iridology, and there appears to be some consistency across multiple disciplines. My archetype seemed to be something not typical, and there appeared to be a common theme: an assumed ability to tap into the mysteries, the downside, that would also make life a bit tricky.

I felt like I could relate to both of those.

Freud or Carl Jung? Dreams were vital to understanding my place in the world. I was already coming to an understanding that fear is what governs all our decisions. Freud seemed so primitive in comparison to Jung and the shadow self. It reaffirmed that the 'demons' I was fighting were my creations. I don't believe that to be entirely true today: in the sense that a demon may be born from you in an energetic state, it's no longer intangible, it then exists. When they exist, people like me can run into them. It was helpful to see a scientific framework that my experiences could relate to; anything that came close to an explanation was welcomed.

My discussions at college and actions in the astral plane/heavens seemed to catch people's attention. Sometimes the best way to test someone is to withhold information, as I had with my Iridology lecturer. Someone decided to test me, without my knowledge. A good idea. I would have.

A close friend of mine was house-sitting for someone. She'd invited my friend and me around for a pool party. The night seemed very normal—until we went to leave. My friend Kat asked if we wanted to see some of the house before we left. We'd spent most of the evening in the area next to the pool. We had no reason to object, so we began the tour.

Nice house. To be honest, I only remember the last room we came to. Kat put her left hand on the door knob and began reaching with her other hand toward where the light switch was on the wall, inside the room. At some point during this action, before her hand hit the switch, I could clearly see an angry old lady. I knew she wasn't physically there; the door wasn't opened more than a couple of inches. Gave me quite the fright, and I immediately said, 'I'm not going in there', in a slightly panicked voice. Then, of course, I realised that would have sounded like a pretty weird reaction for the time and place. Busted for sure.

I'd never seen a ghost outside of my dreams. I'd figured death wasn't the end, from being able to completely leave my body. Seeing one while I was physically awake was new—not going to lie, it scared me a bit. The message from the old lady was pretty clear: don't go in her room.

Kat looked as scared as I felt, and colour drained from her face. My other friend looked like he was just concerned for me—I was visibly anxious. That was the reaction I would expect from someone: a kind of 'What the fuck is going on?' Kat knew something that our other friend and I did not. This all happened within seconds.

I was nervously looking at the floor, turning to go. Kat had already withdrawn her hand and shut the door, looking scared and asking what had happened. At this point, there was no point keeping it to myself. I just wanted to leave, so I told her what I saw and said, 'Just don't go in her room.' Kat's expression had changed. She proceeded to tell me they thought the place was haunted. The owner of the house was a friend of hers; his mother had passed and left him the house. That was her room. That is why she wanted me to 'look around'. Kat wasn't so keen on staying there that night alone with her daughter.

All I could do was assure her that if she stayed away from the room, she would be left alone. Now, I could say a whole heap of information was passed to me—that's how I got the message—but it was far simpler than that. She looked angry when we opened her door. We'd walked throughout the house, and I hadn't even sensed her presence. I hear you, lady!

I let Kat know that she should probably do something, as I imagined spirits like that turn bad over time. Of course, it had never been a concern for me before now. Why hadn't they seen her as well? Remember the butterflies—the passive training in being present. Perhaps. I didn't want to see ghosts while awake, I knew that much.

That experience was my first real lesson on this topic. It forced me to form a practical philosophy about it.

On Ghosts

I saw a great meme once. Two babies are in a womb. One says, 'What do you think happens after birth?' The other replies that they believe nothing exists after birth, it is the end. They then question their sibling on the existence of this 'mum' that they think they hear. It seems obvious when you get here, that it is not the end, and that mum really does exist, but impossible for some from their current perspective.

I think ghosts are aware that I don't have the welcome mat out; the message needs to be important. If you have a ghost making noise in your house, try and resolve why it is there. Deceased family members come to visit, but they don't go bump in the night unless they are stuck. Apart from that, seeing them, awake or asleep, is the same. Like the picture you hold in your mind when you are remembering something: 'Where was the last place I saw my keys?' Picture it. That is the kind of image. Some 'memories' are stronger than others. Why some physically appear is beyond my knowledge, and I have come to realise like many of the experiences, the 'why' doesn't matter.

Movement

Meanwhile, some interesting things were happening while my body slept. This particular experience was a lucid dream that felt like the 'theme' wasn't chosen by me.

I was walking in a desert, wearing a well-worn, tan-coloured Australian army uniform. I had what appeared to be a bolt-action rifle. Approximately fifty meters to my right was another Australian soldier; another fifty meters was another. This was repeated with about ten men. We were doing a sweep for trenches. Orders were to shoot the survivors we found, as we didn't have food or water to spare and we couldn't leave them behind.

It was very hard for me not to stop or interfere with the dream. I don't recall ever having modern warfare dreams. Apart from the dingoes, the only things I'd ever tried to kill in dreams were what I'd perceived as demons—all those times were with sword and fire, probably inspired by the fantasy books I was reading. It just didn't seem like a task I would dream about.

I knew I would find someone. Therefore, I found someone. He was German, and he was scared. He'd thrown down his weapon. Well, I can't kill an unarmed man, but I wasn't ready to end the dream. So I began to cheat. I gave him a jacket the same as ours and told him to go fifty meters to our left—perhaps no one would notice.

Someone noticed. There were a few shouts. Well, I have to get us out of here now, still not wanting to end the dream. A shot was fired. I immediately imagined us inside a mining cart (Indiana Jones inspired). The bullets started hitting and deflecting off the sides as I imagined train tracks into existence, off into the desert. It was only a matter of seconds before I had the focus of mind to realise there was an easier way than continually placing track down with my mind as we sped away—we could fly.

Suddenly, the mining cart had wings: large, white bird wings. That'll do—except no bird wings could carry a metal mining cart. The cart turned into a woven wicker basket as it slowly circled up into the sky. The bullets had stopped, and the soldier I'd rescued was gone. The dream was over?

As I turned back to see where I was going, I was struck by the beauty of the skyline. I'd gone from daytime to twilight. It was like I was on the edge of space—I want to use the word 'firmament', a place between places—and I was no longer alone.

I could see two floating islands. Describing them back then was difficult; now it's simple. They were almost identical to the ones seen in the Avatar movie that aired more than a decade later, minus the vines. The larger of the two floated on the right, and I could not believe what I was seeing.

Dragons. Maybe a dozen of them: chrome, red, olive, and one particularly noticeable black dragon. Definitely the boss. They looked similar to depictions of dragons in movies today. At the time, I wondered if it had come from a description in a book.

While I was processing what I was looking at and noticing the other island has what looks like a house being built on it, I suddenly found myself being dwarfed by the eye of the large black dragon. I can't tell you which of us moved to whom, but I found myself floating—basket was gone—on the edge of space, within an arm's reach of a giant reptile's eye. The slit of the eye was the length of my body. I felt completely naked, like it could literally see straight through me. Its head was huge.

I had a moment of despair, wondering if it was possible to die in this place. Well, if I'm done for, I thought to myself, might as well go down fighting. I drew up my energy and prepared for a fight, similar to what I would do when facing a demon in the astral plane.

Upon doing this, my perspective changed back to where I was. I was back in the basket, and it turned toward the second island. It was a house—was it for me? I woke up.

Had I just tested myself? It was an empowering experience. I felt proud of the decisions I'd made throughout the dream. I also felt like I had someone or something looking out for me in the waking world. After ascending into the sky in the basket, there was a definite point where my lucid dream slipped into something like the place I go when having an out-of-body experience.

Disruption

Things had gotten pretty confusing for me in the dream world. I had not really met any 'friends' at this point. I seemed to be drawn to fighting the bad ones. I'd noticed they weren't really dying. I could stab them or burn them and they would die, but I felt they would come back. This, again, reinforced my thinking that they were my own demons.

I like to believe I was pretty self-aware. I was aware of the mistakes I'd made growing up. I didn't have any grudges, so I wasn't sure what they could be. Then I found a way to get rid of them for good. After a couple of nights of doing my new thing—using blue fire—they weren't coming back.

This wasn't something I did often. I still didn't understand what any triggers may have been for an out-of-body experience. I had trouble relating them to my life most of the time. How would changing the colour of the fire I used completely destroy some emotional demon I'd created? You can't just burn your problems away. Not a pleasant thought to think, maybe they weren't just my undiscovered fears.

I was in the dream world. The ground was like cracked tarmac. I was standing behind a black outcrop of rock—it looked like basalt in color, but was in the form of granite boulders. My best friend from school was on his hands and knees about thirty meters away. He looked exhausted. There was a chain connected to his ankle. Not far from him was an entity I hadn't seen before: a big demon, its attention apparently occupied by my friend.

Well, I thought, I have the element of surprise. So I wasted no time in moving to attack.

A human hand grabbed me on the shoulder. I awoke. I was alone in my room.

That was new. Being woken by someone, having someone 'sneak' up on me, was disturbing. It brought home how cavalier I'd become while still knowing nothing about why, how, or even where I was going. Had my escapades attracted attention?

The answer, I came to understand, was yes. My actions had consequences. When you move through these other realms, especially with force and power, you are not invisible. Destroying entities, even if you believe they are your own demons, sends ripples through that space. It's like setting off fireworks in a quiet forest; it attracts attention from things you might not want to meet and, sometimes, from things that are trying to keep the peace.

Was there 'attention' to grab? Did I just doubt myself to beat my own demon, waking myself in the process? I certainly felt capable in the moment—think about a twenty-three-year-old male who had stood tall in the face of a giant reptile! If something did sneak up on me, it didn't hurt me. If it was a friend, why hadn't it made itself known before?

I'd consumed a lot of literature. While Eastern philosophy hinted at the possibility that this could be more than just a dream, I was lost. I still had no concrete answers. I felt like I understood 'magic', or how to at least make it feel like you could manifest coincidences. The dreams, though, psychology provided no answer.

I felt lonely, and to be honest, for the first time, scared. Seeing a ghost is one thing—there were plenty of stories; even my mother had seen one. I can live with that. Out-of-body experiences, though—it had become too hard to explain. A decade of not knowing what was happening took its toll.

I wanted it to stop. If it were a brain tumour or something, I would probably know by now. What on Earth was going on?

Communication

Feeling deflated and alone on a deep level, I was also physically tired and hungry. Four days at college, four days of work, over four years—it tests your endurance. Thanks to all my friends from those days who invited me for meals!

Due to only being able to afford five subjects a semester in either money or time, enrolling in the clinics became a problem. This ultimately led to a situation where it would take two more years to complete my bachelor's degree. While I enjoyed the content, the rules for practising were pretty loose, mainly due to allopathic medicine (modern medicine) preventing any legitimisation of natural therapies. Imagine denying that food is medicine. The irony, of course, is that they use herbal medicine and the knowledge gathered from herbal medicine to find and isolate active constituents for the drugs they sell. This produces all sorts of unwanted side effects in the majority of cases, it doesn't seem right.

I began 'asking' for it to stop. It didn't take long before I had my first visitor.

I woke. I was lying on my bed in the dream, and I could also see someone standing at the end of my bed. Without thinking, I sprang up to attack, in the process realising a number of things: my safeguards were in place—nothing that wanted to harm me could enter my room, imagined or not. This was an old lady; she seemed familiar, not a threat. My thoughts about repeating my previous methods of 'killing' entities here were ever-present since being woken. The wall of my room was like a window into space, and she quickly exited through it, disappearing once she passed the point of the wall. I remember taking one shot at her as I was thinking this through, in the end, purposely missing. I awoke.

Damn it! Perhaps I could have gotten some answers, even if it was myself explaining it to myself. I was too scared. I was too jumpy. I had lost control of my own dreams. I soon came to believe it was my grandmother whom I had lost when I was young.

I asked again: 'Please make it stop.'

I knew something was listening, I felt like a monkey in the zoo, getting the look of sorrow from the human who wants to help, but is restricted.

Sometime within a week or two, I was in some sort of deserted town. It looked—or should I say felt—like an abandoned mining town. I don't know how big it was. I was inside a single-story house: beige-coloured, dirty-looking walls, with windows you could not see out of properly from the dust and grime of at least a decade of neglect. Colourless cloth hung in pieces for curtains, perhaps blocking less light than the dust. The dust was reddish-brown;

the closer to the ground you looked, the redder and dirtier it was.

The floor inside was worn timber. I was sitting with my back to a wall in what may have been the lounge and kitchen. There was space to my right, although my attention was focused to my left. I could see what I assumed was an entry to a bedroom. Apart from the curtains, this place had nothing: no doors, no furniture, no lighting or fans, not even a sink. But there appeared to be people: two, maybe three. Their clothes seemed to suit the environment: worn and dusty, colours faded. They seemed to be trying to stay quiet, hidden. I felt like they wanted me to stay where I was.

Why would I stay hidden when I could just wake up? Why would I stay hidden when I had become so angry with this stuff I felt I could turn this place into a smouldering pile of ash?

I thought myself to the nearest person, holding them in a position to snap their neck and transferring that intent without the action. I wanted no part of whatever this was. The entity who appeared to be a man had frozen with fear as a result. I woke up.

Sleep was difficult. Why did they appear to be hiding? Why was I with them? I didn't recognise them. How do I make it stop? Only one of those questions was answered.

I asked again: 'Please make it stop'.

Gateways

I found myself lying on my side in an unfamiliar bed—it wasn't mine. Stretching out as far as I could see were countless white beds, each subtly different in design, scattered across a peaceful valley of perfect green grass. No rocks, no bumps, just soft, inviting grass that seemed to go on forever. The beds appeared ordered somehow, though not arranged in neat rows from where I lay.

Standing directly in front of me were three figures: two human-appearing beings wearing what resembled suits, flanking something else entirely. I'm hesitant to use the word 'angel', but that would be the most fitting description, though without wings. The being appeared feminine, taller than the men beside her, a stark contrast in brilliant white that seemed to emanate its own light.

By this stage, I had seen all sorts of things. People could appear however they wanted in these experiences, and frankly, I was done with it all. Without hesitation, I said, 'I don't know you. Go away', and closed my eyes firmly.

I lay there for a moment, thinking about what I had just witnessed. This place felt different—very relaxing, as if real thought had gone into creating it. It wasn't like the gutter realms I seemed to dwell in normally. When I opened my eyes again, everything remained exactly as it was: the beds, the grass valley—all still there. But now only one of the suited men remained; the angel and the other figure had vanished.

You can usually sense when something isn't right, but this place felt genuinely real, wherever it was. I found I wouldn't change a thing about it—or perhaps I couldn't change anything because I had no will to do so.

This place was the answer. All my experiences up to this point—the fighting, the fear, the confusion—had taken place in what I can only describe as the 'gutter realms'. They were chaotic, dense, and close to our own world, filled with fear and lost things. This was different. This was a higher place, a safe harbour, intentionally constructed. I had finally learned that there is a hierarchy to these places, and that if your call is sincere enough, you can be brought to a place where true communication is possible.

Shortly after I opened my eyes, the being before me turned his head to the side, as if looking at someone who wasn't there, and said clearly, 'He's awake'.

This struck me as significant. This was an actual person, I thought—someone in the real world. In these otherworldly places, there's usually no sense of direction, no 'elsewhere' when someone has left your presence. His gesture of turning his head to speak was a pointless action in this realm, something the human mind would do involuntarily. It convinced me of his humanity in a way that nothing else could have.

Suddenly, I was moved. I found myself sitting in a coffee shop near a corner, facing toward the counter. The décor was mostly timber—unremarkable, but comfortable. No one else was there except myself and the three entities I had encountered earlier. There were no cups or anything behind the counter, but the space felt clean and well-used. Most importantly, it felt safe.

The angel now appeared more human. She no longer seemed impossibly tall or glowing with that ethereal light. She had blonde hair and fair skin—I want to say her eyes were blue, but the details feel strangely unclear now, as if the memory of our conversation has been softened at the edges. What remains vivid is the feeling that I could trust her completely.

I know why I was there: I was pleading my case, begging for these experiences to stop. It felt as if I were there for hours, though time moves strangely in such places. Everything happens at the speed of thought, and lifetimes of conversation can occur in moments of real time.

When our conversation finally ended, she looked at me with what I can only describe as gentle certainty and said, 'We will meet again.'

I woke up feeling something I hadn't experienced in a long time: relief. For the first time in months, I slept deeply and peacefully, without fear of where my dreams might take me.

Finding My Off Switch

As the end of the semester approached and many of my friends were finishing or nearly finished their degrees, I decided I would no longer pursue mine. One of my friends was going overseas, and since I had a partner and was staying in Melbourne for the foreseeable future, she asked if I could mind her box of books until her return. I agreed and stored them away, little knowing how symbolic this act would become—putting away one chapter of my life to make room for another.

The most remarkable thing happened after my encounter in the valley: I stopped having out-of-body experiences entirely. But I noticed something else equally strange—I wasn't dreaming at all, or at least not regularly. It appeared to have worked. The angel had somehow honoured my plea.

Being naturally analytical and still wanting to understand what I could, I started paying attention when I would occasionally have a dream. This was a complete flip for me—instead of trying to escape the dream world, I was now studying my rare visits to it. What I discovered was deeply disturbing.

I didn't drink alcohol in those days, having learned its effects on the body, but I did smoke marijuana occasionally. What had changed was my circumstances: I had begun full-time work, had money to spare, and had started smoking regularly. It was during this period that I made a connection that would explain everything.

When I went without cannabis for three or more days, I would start dreaming again. The pattern was unmistakable. When you wake from a dream, as we all know, it can fade incredibly quickly from memory. Dreams operate on short-term memory, which is directly affected by marijuana use. The dreams might have been happening all along, but I simply couldn't remember them; and without the memory, I could sleep peacefully.

Today, we know that smoking marijuana prevents REM sleep, which to me implies you're far less likely to have an out-of-body experience while under its influence. You can still remote view, gain the benefits of meditation, and access other abilities, but there's no walking in the dreams. The off switch I'd been desperately seeking had been there all along, hiding in plain sight.

This revelation raised profound questions that I pondered for months. Had the people in my dreams somehow helped me realise this solution? Was the entire coffee shop encounter just some elaborate experience my brain had conjured while it figured out how to make the experiences stop?

Were the three figures I'd met the same beings from my previous dreams?

Ultimately, these questions no longer mattered. I had found a way to function as a mostly normal human being, and that was worth more than any metaphysical certainty.

During this period, I had an experience that showed me my abilities hadn't disappeared entirely. Near the end of my time studying natural medicine, I found myself in dire financial straits with only twenty dollars to buy a week's worth of food. I could stretch it to maybe last three weeks if I were careful, and I could always ask for help; but pride often overrides common sense.

My younger sister called and asked if I wanted to go out—she was heading to the casino. I wasn't about to let her know how desperate my situation was, so I said yes.

Before leaving, I picked three numbers and held them firmly in my mind. I began noticing these numbers everywhere: on license plates, street addresses, anywhere numbers appeared. I was completely biased toward them, training my consciousness to recognise their patterns. I had done this once before as a test in North

Queensland—it had seemed like just a coincidence then when I'd won around two hundred dollars. Now I needed it to work again. I could do with just a hundred dollars; that would get me out of trouble for the week.

On arrival, I searched for a roulette table where none of my numbers had appeared in the recent draws displayed on the board. I placed my single chip on the first number. It came up immediately. A couple of bets later, the second number hit. After a few more rounds, the third number appeared.

I had a pocket full of cash within about five minutes, and we had just arrived. My sister and her friends had barely managed to get their drinks. Since I no longer had my original numbers to work with, I picked some new ones. They won, too.

I probably had one of the few drinks I'd allow myself that year. The next day, I had enough money to buy the newly released PlayStation and plenty of food to last the week

This experience was a lesson in how to consciously work with the universe. It's about clear, focused intent and tapping into the feeling of needing over wanting. Genuine need, makes it easier…for me.

On Manifestation and Intent

If you want to manifest something, it helps to know it in detail—the smell, the texture, the feeling. You train your consciousness to recognise its pattern, just as I did with the numbers. The universe knows what you want, but it also has a sense of humour: a vague request will get a vague and often ironic answer. But when the request is specific, and the need is real, the synchronicities will align to help you. The trick is to set the intention, then let go and allow the path to appear. I'd like to put in a mention for Rizwan Virk's Simulation Theory. It seems to work very much like a search result—the more specific the better—and the longer you have been looking, the better the results get.

I repeated this process over the years, though I have never tried for a large amount. I would feel like it's too much, or cheating, so it would fail. Know thyself.

This period taught me that finding my 'off switch" 'wasn't about losing my abilities—it was turning the intensity down of my dreams. The marijuana might have quieted the dreams, but it had also taught me something more valuable: that without the extra noise of my dreams, I could still benefit from happy coincidences. Bonus.

I enjoyed my time in Melbourne, but to be fair, I found the winter difficult and, eventually, I was pulled toward the warmth of the sun.

The Road to Understanding

With no real plan for what I would do when I got there, I decided to head back toward the sun and home. I sold everything I couldn't fit in the van I had used for work and hit the road north.

The first night, I drove to West Wyalong, where my parents had bought a motel. The second day brought me to Goondiwindi on the Queensland-New South Wales border. From there, I made the familiar drive to Home Hill, the town where I grew up. I stayed at a friend's house for the night before leaving the next morning to drive the final hour to where I was going to settle. Luckily, I have two sisters, my eldest offering to house me for a time.

The night I stayed in my hometown, something happened. I was having a dream— not an out-of-body experience, just a regular dream, though these often carried messages of their own. I found myself walking along the road beside the Home Hill cemetery. Two young boys were walking beside me.

One seemed happy and carefree, around seven years old, wearing little denim overalls that gave him the look of a farm kid from the 1960s or 70s. He went by the name 'Joey'. The other boy looked troubled, slightly bigger and older than Joey, and clearly bothered by something. Sensing his distress, I asked Joey directly, 'Does he realise he's dead?'

At that question, the bigger boy lunged at me, and I woke with a start.

I had encountered spirits before in my dreams. The best way to describe how talking to spirits works for me is very much like what's depicted in the television show The Medium with Allison DuBois—and some may not realise that show is based on a real person's experiences. To this day, I have only seen one ghost while fully awake, though I've certainly felt their presence many times, as you'll undoubtedly hear about soon enough.

The Missing Child

The day I arrived in Townsville, I saw the second boy—the troubled one from my dream—on television. He was missing and had been for weeks, possibly longer. I had an immediate, sinking feeling that he had met an untimely end.

But what was I supposed to do with this information? Maybe it was just some weird coincidence about coming home. Perhaps I had glimpsed something on TV in Goondiwindi without consciously paying attention, and my subconscious had woven it into a dream. I tried to rationalise it away.

Then I remembered I had left my shoes at my friend's house back in Home Hill. I had to return anyway—maybe I would have a look at the cemetery while I was there, see if Joey was a local resident. Honestly, I had convinced myself I wouldn't find anything significant.

I pulled up on the side of the road where I had been walking with the boys in my dream. Turning off the car, I looked around from where I sat. The cemetery stretched out before me—it could be anywhere among all those graves. In a different section, I could see someone being buried, reminding me that this was a place of ongoing grief and loss.

'What am I doing here?' I muttered to myself.

'This is nuts.'

I started the car, reversed, and began driving back toward the road. Shaking my head at my own stupidity, I made it about fifty meters to a T-intersection—cemetery on my right, cane fields on the left and straight ahead. But the feeling wouldn't leave me alone. I was here now, having driven a hundred kilometres. I might as well have a look.

I turned right and pulled over again, determined to settle this once and for all.

I took only a few steps into the cemetery grounds before coming upon the grave of a boy who had died at six and a half years old in a farming accident in 1967. His name was John.

I don't remember looking at any other graves. My eyes seemed drawn directly to that one headstone. It was a farming district where kids sometimes died in accidents—that was a harsh reality of rural life. The name wasn't Joey, it could still be just a coincidence.

I drove back home with my shoes, but the encounter had left me unsettled.

A Remote Viewing

On the drive back to Townsville, I decided maybe I could look a little further into what had happened to the missing boy. When I got home, I lay down and meditated, picturing the two boys on the road and reaching out to them with my mind. I held the clear intent to understand what had happened to the troubled child.

Suddenly, I found myself sitting in the middle of the back bench seat of an old car—it felt like a station wagon, perhaps an FJ Holden. The paint was faded, either sky-blue or white, and it was nighttime under what seemed like a full or near-full moon. We were driving on what appeared to be a headland surrounded by cane fields.

A house came into view in the distance.

Without hesitation, just knowing I had to get away, I opened the car door while it was still going and ran into the cane fields. I ran about fifty meters along one of the rows before crouching down low, hidden among the tall stalks. Then the impression ended abruptly

This is what I would now confidently call remote viewing. It's a state distinct from an OBE. The vision is often washed out, like a memory, and your conscious mind gets in the way. You have to observe without thinking and analyse it afterwards. I realise now I was practising this unknowingly as a child on long car drives, dozing off and 'flying' next to the car. The movement of the car made it easier to feel the sensation of moving through space, just as I was moved in that vision.

These experiences can be tricky to decipher… who was I going to tell? At the time, there was nothing more I could realistically do with this information.

The gift that wasn't a gift

At some point after settling into my new life in Townsville, I opened the box of books I had been asked to hold for a friend. While I still had the same phone number, I had lost contact with her over the years that had passed.

Among her books, I found exactly what I needed, though I had no idea this book existed or who its author was. It described in precise detail the exact same experiences I had been having while sleeping. Finally, I had confirmation of what was happening to me, it was an OBE.

The book was called Journeys Out of the Body by Robert Monroe. I had been physically given the answers to my questions years before. For the first time since my spiritual experiences had begun, I had a framework for understanding what was happening to me. I wasn't just some isolated person having bizarre dreams—I was part of a broader human experience that others had documented, studied, and learned to navigate.

The irony of claiming 'psychic abilities' while not knowing I was given a book with the answers I searched for in it, is not lost on me. What I assumed happened was, I wanted to move on, I had given up looking for answers so my focus was elsewhere preventing me from feeling the subtle pull to open the box.

Between Roberts book and the debut of the Medium based on Allison DuBois's documented abilities, I was now certain I wasn't crazy. Or maybe I was only a little crazy. But at least I wasn't alone in my particular brand of crazy!

The road to understanding had led me home, not just geographically, but to a place of acceptance and knowledge about my own abilities. I finally knew what to call what I was experiencing; with confidence and, more importantly, I knew I wasn't alone.

When You Think You Can Relax

I'm not sure when the feeling first started. Maybe around the year 2000, or perhaps even earlier, when I began exploring the possibility of past lives. I had this persistent sense that this life was chosen—a conscious return to witness or participate in something important. Humanity has already lived through a few global challenges, and with misunderstood astrology, Mayan calendars, and all sorts of wild prophecies floating around online, the idea that I came back for a kind of

Armageddon didn't feel too far-fetched. If you knew you couldn't truly die in the grand scheme of things, wouldn't massive upheavals in the human timeline be worth coming for? It's like the cosmic fair is in town.

Not that I ever thought it meant the literal destruction of the world—though I wasn't ruling that out. To me, it always meant a monumental change in how we live. And at the time of writing this, I think most of us can feel it: we're at a crossroads.

When I asked the runes about it, the message was 'disruption'. When I asked the tarot, the card was 'Armageddon'. That was concerning. I left it alone for a while, but every time I used the cards or runes, I got the same relentless message. Trouble was brewing. This was around 2013, and the hype of 2000 and 2012 had long passed. I had no dreams of disaster, yet the tools of my intuition were screaming a warning.

Eventually, I did something I rarely do—I decided to ask someone else for a reading. I pulled out the Yellow Pages, found a listing nearby, and went for a drive.

I parked on a busy street near a small business strip. A short walk away, I spotted a sign on the footpath that read 'Tarot Readings'. That had to be the place. I stepped inside a shop where a woman in her sixties, dressed in loose, natural-coloured clothes, greeted me. A man near a bookshelf quickly looked away as I turned toward him, pretending to be absorbed in a book.

To my left was a curtained-off area—the reading room.

'I was hoping to get a reading, if that's okay,' I said.

'Come in.'

We stepped through a heavy blue curtain. The first few cards she drew usually give a reader a sense of a person's archetype. I'd had enough readings to know what to expect, but she didn't react much, just calmly looked them over. Then she paused.

'What does Armageddon mean to you?' she asked.

I froze. The synchronicity of the cards hit me with physical force. I didn't want to answer. I wanted to listen, not share. The silence stretched. I looked down at the floor, feeling like a complete idiot. This wasn't going to be a pleasant, mysterious little reading. It was already too real.

I stood up to leave. To her credit, she gently calmed me down and offered to do a free astrological chart reading instead. A safer topic. She clearly wanted to know more. I don't remember much of that second reading, apart from her interest in the concept of the 'wounded healer'. That was new to me. When it was over, I left, clutching the chart, having barely spoken the entire time—a fact that would surprise anyone who knows me. As I walked out, I checked my phone and saw a message from a friend: 'Busted'. Busted for getting a reading? That didn't bother me. What was funny was that when I got back to my car, I realised I had parked directly outside a sex shop. So much for being 'present'!

For weeks afterwards, it ate away at me. Why had I been so stupid? I was literally asking for help, it was being offered, and I had rejected it. I was scared—scared that I had reached a point where I could no longer laugh this stuff off. Is that why I had not accepted the help offered?

So, I decided to go back. This time, I made sure to park well before I got to the sex shop.

I walked to where I remembered the shop being; but as I approached, I saw the door opened to a staircase leading to a second floor. That wasn't right. I walked closer to the road to get a better view. There it was! A tarot sign, further down the street than I remembered. I headed for it, wondering how I had gotten it so wrong.

But the shop was completely different. A woman named K greeted me. She looked vaguely familiar, but she definitely wasn't the same person.

'Did you change your shop around?' I asked.

'No.'

'Do you have another lady who does readings here?' I pleaded, not wanting to explain everything to someone new.

'No,' she said, looking confused. I probably looked the same. 'I'm sorry, but is there another tarot reader nearby?' I explained I'd been to one just last month.

An Interruption in Time…

A quick break from the story. Today is March 2nd, 2025. Yesterday, I was putting off writing this chapter. It's the weirdest part of my story, and, honestly, it touches on things I'd rather not think about. That same day, an event of global political significance occurred that felt, to me, like watching wolves circle a wounded animal. I felt in my bones that the world had changed.

Later that night, I was hesitant to keep writing this story. I lay down in bed, thinking about what to include, and the

'There used to be someone,' she said, her expression thoughtful. 'She worked out of a shop nearby… upstairs. But that was seventeen years ago.'

I must have looked like a stunned mullet. I had walked past stairs. I remembered shop windows. Had I misremembered that badly? But the meeting felt like it had happened just a month ago. K seemed intrigued by my strange questioning. She confirmed hers was the only shop of its kind in the area, which I verified by walking up and down the street afterwards.

Her reading turned up the usual sort of things, no Armageddon. But I had the distinct feeling that I was meant to help her with something. We talked a bit. She mentioned she'd worked with the police before; so for once, I shared the information I had about the boys from my dreams. By the end of the session, she gave me a set of tarot cards and offered to teach me how to read them—lessons she usually charged for. I told her I already had my own deck, but she insisted.

I didn't speak of this story for over a year. My mind still can't process what happened. There had to be an explanation. I knew I wouldn't learn anything new from K, so I focused on figuring out what I was there to help her with, trying not to think about what had led me there in the first place.

Later, I remembered where I'd seen her before: she used to travel to nearby districts, and I had crossed paths with her in my hometown years ago. But her knowledge was deep. She loved the subject. It was refreshing to talk freely about these things, even if the dogma was a bit much. When I shared stories about making demons go away permanently, she looked shocked and said, 'Only one particular angel can use that.' Dogma again. No matter the source, it seems to block people, for better or worse. Sorry, K, I thought. I'm no angel.

After two weeks of her lessons, she asked me to do a reading for her. The message I got was about a job or a trip over water, and someone giving something up. Nailed it. Her husband, a tugboat driver, had just been offered a job in Gladstone, 800 kilometres away. She would have to close her shop. She didn't look too happy with me. Don't shoot the messenger.

She also told me they had found the boy I'd mentioned a few weeks earlier. He was found in a cornfield, not a cane field. Poor kid. They believed it involved an old, white Toyota Land Cruiser. The view from the back seat would have been similar. The remote viewing made more sense now; you can see how the mind fills in gaps with personal bias. That explains the cane field.

The following week, I was sick and texted her to let her know I couldn't make it. When I showed up the week after, she berated me for not taking things seriously. I explained that I'd messaged her. She claimed she never received it. I pulled out my phone to show her. It turned out the number on her business card was slightly misaligned, making the last digit difficult to discern. It could have been one of two numbers. I got it wrong. Or did I?

There was no doubt in my mind—I had delivered the message I was supposed to. Maybe it was two messages. I politely declined further instruction. Arrogance can make you blind. While I was understandably disturbed by the sequence of events, she had given me a message, too. Very clearly, you could even say loudly.

Finally a Break

By this stage, I was feeling pretty good about it all—not the message about impending doom, but about myself, my gifts. I'd made peace with them. I'd learned how to manage the out-of-body experiences, mostly by smoking marijuana during times of high stress. Most importantly, I finally knew I wasn't alone. There were others like me. That realisation lifted a weight I didn't even know I'd been carrying.

I wish I'd taken the time to write to Robert and thank him for his work before he passed.

The only lingering oddity was that I had a text message and an astrological chart from a place that, as far as I could tell, didn't exist. I parked in different spots each time I went back to see 'K', but I never saw that original shop again. Maybe it was temporary, operating out of someone else's space. A pop-up shop before it was cool. I don't know. But it left me with the feeling that I had to do something.

What could cause   Armageddon? After finishing high school, I had applied for a Bachelor of Environmental Science. Back then, the idea of anthropogenic climate change seemed like the kind of thing that could lead to the global upheaval It made sense—shortages of food and water, droughts, floods, wars. Was it real? I decided to find out. Twenty years had passed since then, and things hadn't improved.

So off I went to university, this time taking out a student loan and working while I studied. Yep, we're definitely causing a problem to our planet. That much was clear.

Now, more comfortable with my experiences, I began sharing my stories more freely, when the moment felt right. My annoying classroom behaviour hadn't improved. I remember one 'Introduction to Science' class where we were given a list of discussion topics. One was: 'Does homeopathy deserve more research?'

Our lecturer was a PhD student. And me? I'm a shaker—I can't help myself sometimes. I knew my input would probably put me in the bad books, but I went for it anyway. I gave a short presentation that included some very real, scientifically verified information, like the Nobel laureate who assembled amino acids into AIDS virus DNA using a homeopathic solution of the virus itself. There's a video about it for anyone interested.

I explained how homeopathy's whole foundation is different: it treats causes, not symptoms. Multiple people with the same illness might need completely different treatments, depending on what caused them to become run down. So, how do you test a treatment for 'the common cold' if the doctor can't even talk to the patient? Zero communication is essential to a double-blind study, and communication with the patient is essential for homeopathy. All you can do is give a generic remedy, and that'll vary by location and environment. It doesn't fit neatly into the double-blind model of testing by its very nature.

Looking back, I could have just been credited for this subject and saved some money. After I spoke, 75% of the class agreed that homeopathy deserved more research. The lecturer? Not happy. They made it harder for me after that. I'm sure I could have found a way to be less combative.

I see how much of my journey was not just about understanding external mysteries, but about navigating my own internal landscape.

On the Ego

The ego—who needs an enemy when you have an ego? This is perhaps the greatest teaching of the 'Know Thyself' path. It's easy to get caught up in the phenomena, in being 'right', or in proving a point. But the real work is in recognising that your own ego can be a far greater obstacle than any external force or sceptical lecturer. The demons you fight in dreams are obvious; the one that whispers in your own mind is harder to spot. True strength isn't just facing dragons; it's mastering the part of yourself that wants to pick a fight in the first place.

University continued. I got bored toward the end I had learned what I came to learn: climate change is real, and it's going to be a problem—probably sooner than we'd like.

was offered a spot in a Master's program in Town Planning, having already completed some coursework at that level. But sitting in an office all day? Joining the IPA? No thanks. At the time, I was working with young men dealing with schizophrenia. I had learned a lot about it during my own search: it was an obvious place for me to look for answers in the beginning. It felt good knowing I could make a difference. I stuck with it—and I still do it today.

Until this point, I hadn't lived with anyone who had a genuine interest in learning. People liked sharing their stories with me—probably because they knew they wouldn't be judged. An essential component to sharing such personal experiences. After finishing uni, I moved in with a mate. We had talked about mysteries before, and he knew from university I was able to think critically.

So when I told him the story about seeing a ghost in Melbourne, he didn't doubt me. He realised there would be no benefit for me to sound crazy. This kind of understanding encouraged me to share.

One night, I was watching a documentary about aliens. Big 'Z'—my housemate—was in his room, opposite mine. I was curious enough to want more than just theories. I was lying on my bed and decided to enter a meditative state. Oddly, I don't even need breathing exercises anymore. I just settle in.

I asked the universe for a sign—if aliens are real, give me a sign.

A moment later, a stack of textbooks on my bedside table crashed to the floor. Made me freeze. Call me a coward: I didn't want to look at first.

From the other room, Big 'Z' shouted, 'What was that?'

His voice probably snapped me out of my shock. I got up, on the opposite side of the bed, and asked him to come out for a cigarette.

When I finally worked up the nerve to look, all the books—four or five of them, decent size text books—were scattered on the floor. I told Big 'Z' what had happened. Talking it through helped. I realised that I probably should've phrased my question better, 'Give me a sign if they are real'. Lesson learned… although I forgot it again later. Any nearby entity could've heard that request. Maybe my spirit guide just has a sense of humour: it wasn't enough to prove aliens were real, knowing already, that other things, like spirits, can go bump in the night. I'm not sure if I ever actually expect something to happen when I 'ask'. Maybe 'K' did have a message for me, 'You don't take it seriously'.

We went back inside and tried to recreate it. I stacked the books as precariously as I could—smallest on the bottom. Most of them were the same size. I rocked the table; it was level. I shook it harder than what could be considered normal. They hardly moved. No reasonable explanation. Now I just have more questions. I'm the one with the answers, supposedly.

Extraterrestrials

I asked one night before bed, after the Russians invaded Ukraine, why 'aliens' did not just destroy all our nukes for us? I woke in the morning to a dream of numerous 'greys' touching my head saying 'the big apple' over and over. I had the impression 'the big apple' was where the decision was made. It was just a dream. It seems unlikely we are alone in the universe, it seems likely 'others' interact with us. It is not however obvious what is going on, and dangerous to hope someone else will come and save us from ourselves.

Now, it's possible that was all just a ruse from Big Z's perspective: he only heard the crash. He had to rely on his trust in me. But naturally, that made him more curious. I shared some more stories. Eventually, we talked about doing some experiments. I was more hesitant than I used to be; but, honestly, it didn't interfere with my life like it used to. I was happy with that.

His curiosity eventually led me to show him something: how I thought weather manipulation —or maybe 'influence' is a better word— worked.

I asked him where he wanted it to rain. He chose his parents' cattle station, which had been in drought. Probably 800 km's away from where we were, I wasn't familiar with the area, which I didn't think was ideal; but I had no idea if it actually made a difference, so I removed the doubt from my mind, try it and see.

I told him to relax and imagine what a storm looked like at home—see the clouds, smell the rain, feel the breeze. As he visualised it, I relaxed and tried to 'find' his thoughts. Sure enough, an image popped into my head. I gave it a little push—felt the air, smelled the scent— and then let it go.

I wouldn't be telling this story if it didn't have an ending.

It rained—good rain—on his parents' property. The neighbours missed out, unfortunately, but at least it wasn't a flood. That was a blessing. 100 mm if I recall. As often happens when something like this occurs, the friendship changed. People struggle to explain it. Denying it happened is easier if I'm not around. And accepting that these things are possible usually requires a bit of solitude.

On the Weather

Just don't, unless it's an emergency. Thinking you can control the weather is absolutely bonkers. You either think you do, and you don't, which makes you crazy; or you think you do and you do, which will also make you crazy. You should probably not write a book and talk about it.

The butterfly effect is a real concern. It's a scientific term, it suggests a butterfly that flaps its wings can end up creating a storm, in its most extreme case. You are disturbing a balance. If you take moisture out of the air, the rain doesn't fall somewhere else; that is the least of the problems you can cause. Playing a game where the rules are not crystal clear should be done with caution.

This was a difficult but necessary lesson. Sharing an experience like this is not like sharing a story; it's like handing someone a piece of a world they didn't know existed. It can be a heavy gift. The kind people may think they want, as it seems like power, but it is isolating. I imagine that's why most Shamans live alone.

On Shared Experiences
and Their Consequences

When you directly involve someone in a paranormal event, you are forcibly rewriting their reality. Their world had a set of rules, and you've just shown them those rules are incomplete. For some, this is exciting. For many, it's terrifying. It's often easier for them to question their relationship with you than to question their entire understanding of the universe. The distance that grows isn't necessarily a rejection of you; it's a necessary period of retreat for them to process a fundamental shock to their system. The result is usually the same, the friendship is lost within a short period of time.

What's Next

For me, yoga, Thai Chi. I'm turning fifty this year. Combining meditation with exercise seems like cheating in regards to re-connecting. It is such a beneficial practice. I'm hoping it helps me further my connection, which I have not worked on for decades. At the beginning of this book I was smoking cigarettes and pot, now I smoke neither, my dreams are returning and the synchronicities occur on a regular basis.

I hope that this book will help someone like me. Perhaps your child is going through some interesting experiences, and my stories can help them. Perhaps you are like me, and just need that reassurance that you aren't having a breakdown or dealing with a brain tumour or something. I am aiming to reconnect, and I would like to help others find a connection or establish one they lost. This is a part of who we are; we no longer, or perhaps have never, fully understood our connection to our surroundings. I would like to collaborate with people who see the world today and can "dream" of solutions. Share your stories, don't be afraid like I was. It's taken me decades to stop writing these synchronicities off. I hope you don't mind, but one more story…..

My daughter had been going to kindergarten for about a month. At the time, she often mentioned a life 'when she was older', and spoke of a sister (who was an actual friend, not a biological one), and referred to her 'other mum'. Confusing, I know. She has never mentioned her other dad, oddly. She came home one day, and, as usual, I asked how her day had been.

'I cried today,' she said, looking down.

'What happened, sweetie?' I inquired. This wasn't unusual either—heart of gold and a little temper that will melt that gold to balance it all out.

'My sister and I were crying together in the sandpit,' she replied.

'Okay,' I said encouragingly. 'What made you cry?'

'When we were sisters, we drowned. We were the last two on the boat.'

Immediately, I saw the girl on the boat, in the storm—the girl who led me to my family trees. I hadn't thought of that for decades. It doesn't even fit the description that well, but it was a vivid recollection in that moment, and I was present to acknowledge it. We didn't inquire further, as she loves the 'stage' and it can quickly turn into attention-seeking. We just try to listen, be present—no easy task in the modern world. Pulling on the roots of a plant doesn't make it grow faster either, and people grow in their own time. Just nurture it—one of the hardest lessons I have had to learn as a parent and support worker.

Help me reprogram the future with our thoughts and our shared connection. After all, it's not necessary to leave your body to connect to the divine. The path is less important than the destination. I believe that becomes obvious over time. So pray, meditate, perform rituals, and use caution. Spiritual growth is personal—do it your way; but let's do it together. Make a positive dream, then spread the positive dream, let people know that what seems like a disaster is actually a chance for something special, we can do better than the path we are currently on!

To me, it's not the practice that's important, not the funny hat, or the stick you might carry, not the words, not the place, nor the time. It just is. To be perfectly clear, 'it is what it is' Nothing more, nothing less. It's just…there. All you need do is ask.

I wish to welcome all beliefs. It does not matter how people reach 'God'. No one owns it. We only own the path we chose to get there.

Conclusion

Awakening is not a pleasant experience from my perspective. It is certainly not for everyone, perhaps if you sort it out, rather than feel like it was forced on you, things would be easier, but some side effects can't be avoided. People won't understand you, my family accepts me, as I am, but I have lost many friends. Not because I don't like them, but because they don't know themselves, and you learn quickly, most people aren't ready to learn why they repeat behaviours that damage their lives. Accepting loss may be easier, because when you know yourself well, isolating the feelings, breaking them down and knowing what is yours and what is projected, protects you in a way from those whom would do you harm, most people are oblivious to the harm they cause, knowing this makes it simpler to forgive.

As a result, get to know yourself, by whatever means you have at hand, runes, tarot, study, deep conversation, meditation, divination tools….living life and being present. Never make the goal to be awakened, or enlightened, the "seeker" is also known as the "fool" this is particularly the case when the seeking is done externally, answers will come when they are ready, pulling the roots of a plant does not make it grow faster, but can disrupt the process.

My conclusion is that we live many lives, our body is a vehicle, and 'we' are the pilot. Everything we see is built up of interacting energies. 'Here' the world we see, is the culmination of our combined consciousness. We are like a computer or phone, a node, that interacts with a much greater entity or field. You may have heard something like this before, or just come to the same conclusion. From my perspective, having had the experiences I have had, it's the only conclusion that makes sense. Science is getting close. My experiences will never be 'proof' for someone else, but many of you will be able to relate to one of the stories I have shared. We all have those weird moments. I have trouble convincing myself, and that's why I named the book 'Give me a sign'. I'm just like you, something weird happens, and then I question it, or I might ask for a sign, get one, and then pretend I didn't. I'm generally sceptical when others share their experiences, as we all should be to a degree. Growth is personal. I don't want to ignore this sign. I don't have any claim as some spiritual guide, or some kind of prophet but I don't want to regret keeping it to myself. We need to come together, spiritually, no matter our belief system. The division has turned people away from their traditional beliefs, along with scandals. Let people tap in however they choose, most of us want to live in peace, let's focus on that.

What do you think? Was 'K' right? Publishing my story seems like I'm finally taking it seriously. We should all be comfortable enough to accept our spirituality, our connection. Change is coming, quicker than some realise; it can be good, or bad. We need to believe, we need to listen to that little voice telling us, things are not right.

Let's debate what 'dream' would help make our time here more productive on a spiritual level. We have a chance to focus human resources on something special. We are all being given the chance to decide. Whether we realise it or not, we are programming our future, with our dreams and physically with AI. Are we brave enough to take a chance? Do we have the will to shape it? A future worth talking about. Join me in these thoughts, discussions, dreams, and actions. Some say 111's can make dreams come true, I don't see why we can't test that theory?

If this book has your spidey senses tingling, your chi flowing, your belief in God strengthened, filling you with divine light, share it. We are the broken up magnet, a lot stronger together. This moment in time will define human evolution. Let us make it a positive one.

Epilogue

J oin me in a discussion, I'm not a leader, I'm a dreamer. Lets discuss 'reality', and how we can change it. I can see a bright future, and I can see many dystopian futures. These are the thoughts of us all, mingling in the great consciousness that permeates all things. We need to shine the light on the positives, on the possibilities worth living for. The current world order does not want that, they want division and control, as always. With the advent of AI, this makes them closer to becoming insurmountable at the cost of all the innocent souls who just want to live in peace. I'm not OK with that.

Hope is not lost, it's been drowned in advertising. Spirituality isn't dead, it's been drowned in dogma. People say, Utopian futures are not possible, is that true? Or are we programmed to believe that. Think about it, should we try for some sort of Utopia and fall short, or accept the dystopian futures handed to us?

There is not scarcity of food and shelter, that is a direct result of greed. The same for medical cures. Planned obsolescence is real, things are built to break, so we 'need' to buy another, people are convinced they need the newest model, which is usually so similar most people can't tell the difference. It's a form of induced madness. There are no wars if we, the people, don't pick up a gun or build the weapons. AI has changed that, so we need to build an AI based on principles rather than hard restraints. Models built on current data are corrupted by capitalistic views of what is possible. We can move away from that. That is just one aspect.

I'm no fan of the big orange guy, but he has done something that seemed impossible, he has reminded the world of the dangers we face, he has shaken the pillars that held up our current systems. He has given us all a chance to make serious changes. It doesn't matter your belief system, it doesn't matter what 'end of the world scenario' you think may occur or not occur. We are in this together, and I'm not afraid to try and make the world a better place, so come, join the discussion, come with solutions, come with problems, come with questions and let's see if we can get this ship back on course.

As I came to the end of writing this memoir, if that fits, I revisited some old tools I used to use. One in particular I used to use, or feel a connection with was Astrology. The connection was not out of experiences, like 'wow, that was really accurate', in fact I always found it was at best 50% accurate, but out of the principle behind it.

Everything we know of is made of energy, the chair I'm sitting on, to the thoughts in my head. All those bits and pieces came from the stars at some time in the past, and we know now that quantum physics means distance does not mean separation. The stars, their positions, have an influence, they push and pull each other, we even see the moon's effect on the oceans; the effects may be subtle but they are there. As a result, I revisited Astrology. As I mentioned earlier, my star sign was complicated. I realise now everyone is. We are a tapestry, woven from energy.

The result of this, was to dive deeply into producing my own reading. I looked past just the standard Natal chart—which can be overwhelming without learning what all the trines, squares, and houses mean—and focused on the profound similarities between different astrological systems. A detailed natal chart interpretation, focusing on who you are, what drives you, your soul purpose, without the barrier of the terms used, makes a very useful tool.

I had no idea I was going to build this when I began writing, but after mapping out my own chart and being shocked by the accuracy, I felt other people might find it useful too.

I created an astrological planner called The Weaver's Almanac, a framework that weaves together Western, Vedic, and Chinese astrology. It is not a fortune-telling device meant to predict your future. Rather, it is a practical tool I found useful for understanding the subtle energies affecting our daily lives, and ultimately, just one more way to help us all "Know Thyself".

About the Author

Justin Nichols has spent his life navigating the space between the ordinary and the extraordinary. With a trade as Printing Machinist, knowledge of natural therapies and a bachelors degree in Environmental science, he currently works in mental health support in North Queensland, Australia. Give Me a Sign is his first book.